Dinosaurs Alive!

Brachiosaurus

and Other Dinosaur Giants

Jinny Johnson

Illustrated by Graham Rosewarne

A+

Smart Apple Media

Published by Smart Apple Media
2140 Howard Drive West
North Mankato, MN 56003

Designed by Helen James
Edited by Mary-Jane Wilkins
Artwork by Graham Rosewarne

Printed in China

Library of Congress Cataloging-in-Publication Data

Johnson, Jinny.
Brachiosaurus and other dinosaur giants / by Jinny Johnson.
p. cm. — (Dinosaurs alive!)
Includes index.
ISBN 978-1-59920-065-1
1. Brachiosaurus—Juvenile literature. I. Title.

QE862.S3J636 2007
567.913—dc22   2006102835

First Edition

9 8 7 6 5 4 3 2 1

Photographs by Louie Pslhoyos/CORBIS, James L.Amos/CORBIS

Contents

A dinosaur's world

A dinosaur was a kind of reptile that lived millions of years ago. Dinosaurs lived long before there were people on Earth.

We know about dinosaurs because many of their bones and teeth have been discovered. Scientists called paleontologists (pay-lee-on-ta-loh-jists) learn a lot about the animals by studying these bones.

The first dinosaurs lived about 225 million years ago. They disappeared—became extinct— about 65 million years ago.

Some scientists believe that birds are a type of dinosaur, so they say there are still dinosaurs living all around us!

Amargasaurus

TRIASSIC
248 to 205 million years ago
Some dinosaurs that lived at this time:
Coelophysis, Eoraptor, Liliensternus,
Plateosaurus, Riojasaurus, Saltopus

EARLY JURASSIC
205 to 180 million years ago
Some dinosaurs that lived at this time:
Crylophosaurus, Dilophosaurus, Lesothosaurus,
Massospondylus, Scelidosaurus, Scutellosaurus

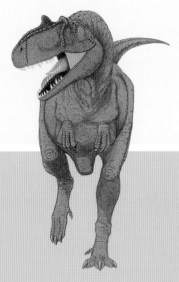

LATE JURASSIC
180 to 144 million years ago
Some dinosaurs that lived at this time: Allosaurus,
Apatosaurus, Brachiosaurus, Ornitholestes,
Stegosaurus, Yangchuanosaurus

Allosaurus

EARLY CRETACEOUS
144 to 98 million years ago
Some dinosaurs that lived at this time: Baryonyx, Giganotosaurus,
Iguanodon, Leaellynasaura, Muttaburrasaurus,
Nodosaurus, Sauropelta

LATE CRETACEOUS
98 to 65 million years ago
Some dinosaurs that lived at this time:
Ankylosaurus, Gallimimus, Maiasaura, Triceratops,
Tyrannosaurus, Velociraptor

Triceratops

Brachiosaurus

Can you believe there was once an animal
that weighed more than 12 elephants?
It was the brachiosaurus, one of the largest,
heaviest creatures that ever lived.

The brachiosaurus was one of a group of
giant, plant-eating dinosaurs called sauropods.
These huge, long-necked dinosaurs were the
biggest land animals ever.

This is how you say
brachiosaurus:
brak-ee-oh-sore-us

Brachiosaurus's name means "arm lizard." Its front legs are much longer than its back legs. This was unusual among sauropods.

BRACHIOSAURUS

Group: sauropods (sauropoda)

Length: up to 98 feet (30 m)

Lived in: North America, Africa, Europe

When: Late Jurassic, 155–140 million years ago

The brachiosaurus had a huge body and a long, heavy tail. A fully grown brachiosaurus may have weighed an amazing 77 tons (70 t).

Dinosaurs lived long before there were people on Earth. But here you can see how big a dinosaur was compared to a seven-year-old child.

Inside a brachiosaurus

An animal the size of a brachiosaurus
needed strong bones to carry
its great weight.

The brachiosaurus's neck contained 15 bones.
Its ribs were longer than an adult human, and
its leg bones were thick and heavy. Only its
head was small. It measured about 2.5 feet
(75 cm)—about the same as a horse's head.

No one knows why sauropods, such as
the brachiosaurus, were so big, but their
huge size may have helped them
in two ways.

*The brachiosaurus had big, fleshy feet
with five toes. There were large claws
on the first toe of each front foot and
on the first three toes of each back foot.*

8

First, big animals are hard to attack.
Few other dinosaurs could win against
a fully grown sauropod.

Second, the larger an animal is, the
more food it can easily reach.

*A brachiosaurus's
strong bones easily
supported its
enormous body.*

*This dinosaur's
huge front legs
were more than
13 feet (4 m)
long.*

9

A brachiosaurus in action

This enormous animal fed only on plants. Scientists once thought it could reach up into the highest trees, but they now think that sauropods may not have been able to lift their heads very high after all.

A brachiosaurus would still have been able to reach higher than most dinosaurs because of its long front legs. It could take big mouthfuls of fresh, green leaves from taller trees that other dinosaurs could not reach.

A brachiosaurus may have eaten as much as a ton of plant food every day. It chopped the leaves from plants with its spoon-shaped teeth.

10

Fossilized dinosaur footprints show that sauropods, such as the brachiosaurus, moved around in groups called herds. But the dinosaurs were so big and heavy that they couldn't move very fast.

Baby brachiosaurs

Like most dinosaurs, the brachiosaurus laid eggs. The female probably laid as many as 100 eggs, each the size of a football.

Once a female brachiosaurus laid her eggs, she left them to hatch by themselves.

A sauropod egg had a hard shell to protect the baby dinosaur growing inside.

The newly hatched baby sauropods were very small compared to their giant parents, and they had to watch out for meat-eating dinosaurs. A baby sauropod made a tasty meal for a hungry predator.

Baby sauropods probably stayed together in groups for safety.

Diplodocus

This mighty dinosaur, with its long neck and whip-like tail, was one of the longest land animals that has ever lived.

The diplodocus had bones that were partly hollow, so it was much lighter than the brachiosaurus. The diplodocus weighed only about 12 tons (11 t).

The diplodocus had a small head and rows of teeth like little pegs. The teeth looked thin and weak, but they were just right for stripping leaves from ferns, the animal's favorite food.

The diplodocus could not chew, but it may have swallowed stones to help grind down the food in its stomach.

DIPLODOCUS

Group: sauropods (sauropoda)

Length: up to 85 feet (26 m)

Lived in: North America

When: Late Jurassic, 155–145 million years ago

This is how you say diplodocus: dip-plo-doh-kus

Dinosaur experts think that the diplodocus held its long tail off the ground as it walked.

Camarasaurus

The camarasaurus was smaller than the brachiosaurus and diplodocus, and it had a shorter neck and tail.

Many of the camarasaurus's bones were hollow, so it was lighter than some of its relatives, but it still probably weighed as much as 22 tons (20 t). It had large nostrils on the top of its broad head.

The camarasaurus lived at about the same time as the diplodocus. But its bigger teeth meant that it could eat tougher plants than the diplodocus, so the two dinosaurs did not eat the same food.

The camarasaurus lived in herds. The younger dinosaurs stayed close to the adults where they were safe from predators.

CAMARASAURUS

Group: sauropods (sauropoda)

Length: 75 feet (23 m)

Lived in: North America

When: Late Jurassic, 150–140 million years ago

This is how you say camarasaurus: kam-ar-a-sore-us

The camarasaurus's large feet had five toes. The inner front toe on each foot had a sharp, curved claw.

17

Apatosaurus

The apatosaurus was another huge sauropod.
It was not quite as long as the diplodocus, but it
was much heavier, weighing up to 38 tons (34 t).

Few creatures would attack
a gigantic animal like this.
But if a hungry tyrannosaur
approached, the apatosaurus
lashed out with its long tail.
The tail probably made a
cracking sound like a whip
to warn off enemies.

This is how you say
apatosaurus:
ah-pa-toh-sore-us

If an attacker came
near, a blow from a
sauropod's tail could
break its legs with
one stroke.

APATOSAURUS

Group: sauropods (sauropoda)

Length: up to 69 feet (21 m)

Lived in: North America

When: Late Jurassic, 154–145 million years ago

A sauropod's long tail was its only weapon against attackers.

Mamenchisaurus

This sauropod had one of the longest necks of any animal ever. It made up about half of the animal's length and had 19 long neck bones.

A giraffe's long neck measures six feet (1.8 m) and contains just seven neck bones.

Dinosaur experts once thought that the mamenchisaurus could reach high to feed on leaves from the tops of trees, just like giraffes do today. But now they think that the dinosaur could not lift its head very high after all—just enough to reach out for food.

The mamenchisaurus was too big to move around in areas of thick forest. But with its long neck, it could reach in and feed on leaves.

MAMENCHISAURUS

Group: sauropods (sauropoda)

Length: up to 72 feet (22 m)

Lived in: China

When: Late Jurassic, 155–145 million years ago

This is how you say mamenchisaurus: mah-men-kee-sore-us

Seismosaurus

This giant dinosaur was one of the longest land animals ever. It was 131 feet (40 m) from its nose to the tip of its long, whip-like tail.

The name seismosaurus means "earth-shaking lizard." Like other sauropods, this dinosaur moved in herds, feeding on plants. Its long neck helped it reach food all around so it didn't have to move far.

The seismosaurus and most other sauropods probably lived for 100 years or more.

This is how you say seismosaurus: size-moh-sore-us

SEISMOSAURUS

Group: sauropods (sauropoda)

Length: 131 feet (40 m)

Lived in: North America

When: Late Jurassic, 155–144 million years ago

Amargasaurus

The amargasaurus was a small sauropod.
It is named after a canyon called La Amarga
in Argentina where its bones were first found.

The amargasaurus had two rows of spines along its backbone, from neck to tail. These may have been covered with skin, making the dinosaur look larger to scare predators. Or the spines may have helped protect it from attackers.

AMARGASAURUS

Group: sauropods (sauropoda)

Length: up to 39 feet (12 m)

Lived in: Argentina

When: Early Cretaceous,
132–127 million years ago

This is how you say amargasaurus:
ah-marg-ah-sore-us

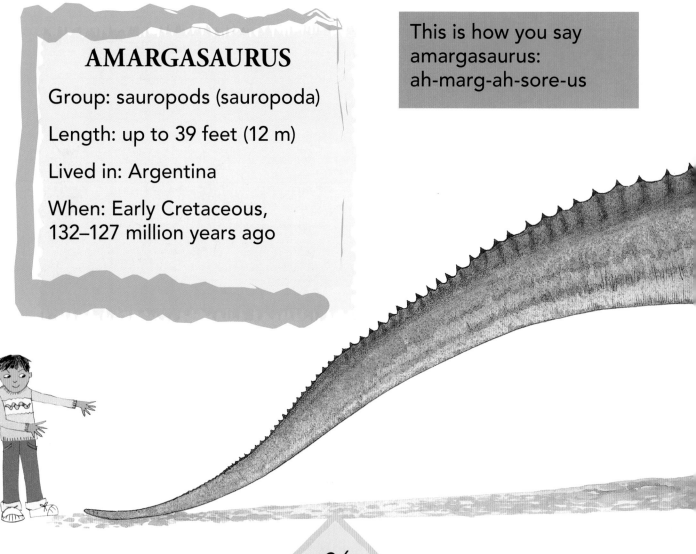

Dinosaur experts think that sauropods may have stood on two legs to reach food or frighten off an enemy.

Alamosaurus

This was one of the last of the sauropods. It lived in North America at a time when most sauropods had already died out.

The alamosaurus belonged to a group of sauropods called titanosaurs. These dinosaurs had shorter tails than the brachiosaurus and tough scales covering their skin. This body armor may have helped protect them from predators.

ALAMOSAURUS

Group: sauropods (sauropoda)

Length: up to 69 feet (21 m)

Lived in: North America

When: Late Cretaceous, 70–65 million years ago

26

The alamosaurus had a small head and lots of small slender teeth for stripping leaves from plants.

This is how big a sauropod footprint looks next to a human footprint.

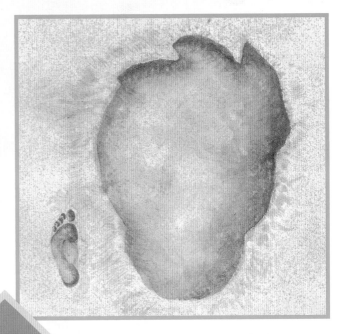

This is how you say alamosaurus:
ah-la-mow-sore-us

Discovering dinosaurs

Dinosaurs lived long ago—millions
of years before the first people. So how
do we know so much about them?

One way is by comparing them with similar
animals today. Dinosaur experts also learn from
fossils such as bones, teeth, and eggs. Teeth
give clues about what the animals ate. Marks on
bones show where muscles were attached and
help scientists figure out the animal's shape.

*This fossilized skull
of a horned dinosaur
called protoceratops
was found in the
Gobi Desert in
Mongolia.*

A fossil is something that has turned into rock over millions of years. It could be a bone or a tooth. When an animal dies, the soft parts of its body rot away or are eaten by other animals. The hard parts are left. Sometimes these may be buried in mud, a river, or a lake bed.

Over millions of years, minerals in the water and mud seep into the bones or teeth and replace the original bone. The bones stay the same shape, but gradually become more like rock than bone.

A paleontologist slowly removes some huge sauropod bones from rocks in Utah.

Words to know

Carnivore
An animal that eats other animals.
The tyrannosaurus was a carnivore.

Fossils
Parts of an animal such as bones and teeth that
have been preserved in rock over millions of years.

Herbivore
An animal that eats plants. The brachiosaurus was
an herbivore.

Herd
A group of animals that usually moves and feeds together.

Paleontologist
A scientist who looks for and studies fossils to learn
more about the creatures of the past.

Predator
An animal that lives by hunting and killing
other animals.

Reptile
An animal with a backbone and a dry scaly body.
Most reptiles lay eggs with leathery shells.
Dinosaurs were reptiles. Today's reptiles include
lizards, snakes, and crocodiles.

Sauropods

A group of long-necked, plant-eating dinosaurs that includes the largest dinosaurs known.

Tyrannosaur

A type of large, meat-eating dinosaur, such as the tyrannosaurus, that attacked plant-eating dinosaurs.

Index